Name

Copyright and Legal

Copyright

Legal and Disclaimer

This planner should not be considered a legally binding document. It is recommended you consult with a lawyer to create a formal, legally binding will regarding your desired final wishes and arrangements should you become incapacitated, or upon passing.

The author, publisher, and all those involved in the creation of this workbook, under any and all circumstances, are not considered responsible or liable for any damages that come from its content or purchase. Use of this planner is meant entirely for the benefit of the purchaser in the organization and documentation for end of life wishes and preferences.

It is a good idea to ensure those involved in your end of life planning and arrangements are notified of this document and its location. Important, sensitive and private content such as personal identification information and passwords are included in the following pages, and it is essential this information not become misplaced to avoid the risk of identity theft or misuse of any kind.

The owner and users of this document takes full responsibility for the safekeeping, accuracy, and content upon use. The user agrees this planner is considered an organizational workbook only, in which to record final wishes and desires relevant in the case of incapacitation or upon passing.

Table of Contents

Introduction

Welcome to your Peace of Mind and Heart Planner. This book is designed to make life-planning as simple, user friendly, and stress-free as possible.

Your Planner is a comprehensive, customizable, all-in-one workbook to record your vital information, personal wishes, and final messages to loved ones.

It is a valuable gift for those left behind so that they can ensure your instructions are fulfilled accordingly, and to help avoid duress or confusion by planning in advance.

We have provided plenty of space to customize each section as per your needs, and include additional overflow space at the back of the book if required. It is wise to begin with the initial personal identification section first, and then proceed to one chapter at a time, collecting all the documentation and information in advance for efficiency sake.

Remember to update this planner as changes to your circumstances arise, such as new employment, investments, insurance, or adjustments to your personal wishes.

Please remember, this planner is not considered a legal document and should not be considered a formal will.

*Always store this workbook somewhere safe, to prevent sensitive, private information from getting into the wrong hands.

Personal Information

My Legal Name

_____

_____

Address

_____

_____

_____

Mailbox or P.O. Box Number

_____

_____

Mailbox Location

_____

Key Location

_____

Primary Phone Numbers

_____

_____

_____

_____

Family Members and Dependents

Spouse's Name / Maiden Name

_____

_____

Children's Names

_____

_____

_____

_____

_____

_____

Grandchildren's Names

_____

_____

_____

_____

_____

_____

_____

_____

_____

Family Members and Dependents

Additional Dependents Names

Pets Names

Notes

Family Members and Dependents

Siblings Names

_____

_____

_____

_____

_____

Mother's Name / Maiden Name

_____

_____

Father's Name

_____

_____

Ex-Spouse's Name/s

_____

_____

_____

Notes

_____

_____

_____

_____

At The Time of My Passing

Please Contact the Following People upon My Passing or Incapacity

Spouse / Partner

Name

Contact Information

Notes

Healthcare Power of Attorney Agent

Name

Contact Information

Notes

Executor

Name

Contact Information

Notes

Please Contact the Following People Upon My Passing or Incapacity

Family and Close Friends

Name

Contact Information

Relationship

Name

Contact Information

Relationship

Name

Contact Information

Relationship

Name

Contact Information

Relationship

Name

Contact Information

Relationship

Name

Contact Information

Relationship

Please Contact the Following Family, Friends, and Associates

Name

Relationship

Contact Information

Name

Relationship

Contact Information

Name

Relationship

Contact Information

Name

Relationship

Contact Information

Name

Relationship

Contact Information

Name

Relationship

Contact Information

Please Contact the Following People Upon My Passing or Incapacity

Name

Relationship

Contact Information

Name

Relationship

Contact Information

Name

Relationship

Contact Information

Name

Relationship

Contact Information

Name

Relationship

Contact Information

Name

Relationship

Contact Information

Please Contact the Following People Upon My Passing or Incapacity

Name

Relationship

Contact Information

Name

Relationship

Contact Information

Name

Relationship

Contact Information

Name

Relationship

Contact Information

Name

Relationship

Contact Information

Name

Relationship

Contact Information

Please Contact the Following People Upon My Passing or Incapacity

Name

Relationship

Contact Information

Name

Relationship

Contact Information

Name

Relationship

Contact Information

Name

Relationship

Contact Information

Name

Relationship

Contact Information

Name

Relationship

Contact Information

Please Contact the Following People Upon My Passing or Incapacity

Name

Relationship

Contact Information

Name

Relationship

Contact Information

Name

Relationship

Contact Information

Name

Relationship

Contact Information

Name

Relationship

Contact Information

Name

Relationship

Contact Information

Please Contact the Following People Upon My Passing or Incapacity

Name

Relationship

Contact Information

Name

Relationship

Contact Information

Name

Relationship

Contact Information

Name

Relationship

Contact Information

Name

Relationship

Contact Information

Name

Relationship

Contact Information

Please Contact the Following People Upon My Passing or Incapacity

Name

Relationship

Contact Information

Name

Relationship

Contact Information

Name

Relationship

Contact Information

Name

Relationship

Contact Information

Name

Relationship

Contact Information

Name

Relationship

Contact Information

Place of Worship: *Church, Synagogue, Etc.*

Name #1

Contact Information

Name #2

Contact Information

Notes

Lawyer #1

Name

Contact Information

Notes

Lawyer #2

Name

Contact Information

Notes

Estate Planner

Name

Contact Information

Notes

Additional Key Contact Information

Business Employer / Associate

Company and Agent Name

Contact Information

Business Employer / Associate

Company and Agent Name

Contact Information

Business Employer / Associate

Company and Agent Name

Contact Information

Financial Advisor

Company and Agent Name

Contact Information

Financial Advisor

Name

Contact Information

Accountant

Company and Agent Name

Contact Information

Additional Key Contact Information

Health Care Provider – Medical

Company and Agent Name

Contact Information

Health Care Provider – Dental

Company and Agent Name

Contact Information

Health Care Provider – Vision

Company and Agent Name

Contact Information

Health Care Provider – Other

Company and Agent Name

Contact Information

Veterinarian

Company and Agent Name

Contact Information

Veterinarian

Company and Agent Name

Contact Information

Additional Key Contact Information

Other

Name

Contact Information

Name

Contact Information

Name

Contact Information

Name

Contact Information

Name

Contact Information

Name

Contact Information

Name

Contact Information

Name

Contact Information

Contact Information - Notes

Funeral Arrangements

Funeral Arrangements Contact Person

Name

Relationship

Church, Synagogue, Other

Name of Priest, Rabbi, Other

Contact Information

Funeral Home

Address

Contact Information

Cemetery or Crematorium

Plot / Address

Contact Information

Funeral Insurance Policy

Company Name

Contact Information

Notes

Burial

Headstone Details _____

_____

_____

_____

Cremation

Ashes to be spread _____

_____

_____

_____

Obituary

Please Include the Following _____

_____

_____

_____

_____

_____

_____

_____

_____

Please Include the Following Personal Message to My Loved Ones

Funeral Arrangements - Notes

Asset Overview - What My Loved Ones Can Expect

Note: *Please see will for detailed instructions and division of assets.*

Personal Residence Address

_____

_____

_____

PO Box Location and Address

_____

_____

Partner / Co-Owner Names

_____

_____

Contact Information

_____

_____

Legal Documentation Location and Instructions

_____

_____

_____

_____

Assets Overview

Keys Location and Miscellaneous Instructions

_____

_____

Alarm and Security Information

_____

_____

Utilities Warranties and Documentation Location

_____

_____

_____

Upkeep Information and Document Location (Gardener, Etc.)

_____

_____

_____

Notes

_____

_____

_____

_____

_____

_____

_____

Assets Overview

Investment Property / Second Home Address

_____

_____

_____

Type of Property (Residential / Commercial)

_____

_____

PO Box Location and Address

_____

_____

Partner / Co-Owner Names

_____

_____

Contact Information

_____

_____

Legal Documentation Location and Instructions

_____

_____

_____

Assets Overview

Keys Location and Miscellaneous Instructions

_____

_____

Alarm and Security Information

_____

_____

Utilities Warranties and Documentation Location

_____

_____

_____

Upkeep Information and Document Location (Gardener, Etc.)

_____

_____

_____

Notes

_____

_____

_____

_____

_____

_____

Assets Overview

Vehicle List: *Car, Motorcycle, Recreation Vehicle, Snowmobile, Etc.*

Vehicle

Year/Make/Model

VIN – ID

Ownership Documentation Location

Lease / Load Information

Keys Location

Notes

Vehicle

Year/Make/Model

VIN – ID

Ownership Documentation Location

Lease / Load Information

Keys Location

Notes

Assets Overview

Vehicle List:

Vehicle _____

Year/Make/Model _____

_____

VIN – ID _____

Ownership Documentation Location _____

Lease / Load Information _____

Keys Location _____

Notes _____

_____

_____

_____

Vehicle _____

Year/Make/Model _____

_____

VIN – ID _____

Ownership Documentation Location _____

Lease / Load Information _____

Keys Location _____

Notes _____

_____

_____

_____

Vehicle List:

Vehicle _____

Year/Make/Model _____

_____

VIN – ID _____

Ownership Documentation Location _____

Lease / Load Information _____

Keys Location _____

Notes _____

_____

_____

_____

Vehicle _____

Year/Make/Model _____

_____

VIN – ID _____

Ownership Documentation Location _____

Lease / Load Information _____

Keys Location _____

Notes _____

_____

_____

_____

Investments: Stocks, Mutual Funds, and Other

Type _____

Location _____

Account Number _____

Contact Person _____

Documentation Location _____

Notes _____

_____

Type _____

Location _____

Account Number _____

Contact Person _____

Documentation Location _____

Notes _____

_____

Type _____

Location _____

Account Number _____

Contact Person _____

Documentation Location _____

Notes _____

_____

Investments: Stocks, Mutual Funds, and Other

Type _____

Location _____

Account Number _____

Contact Person _____

Documentation Location _____

Notes _____

_____

Type _____

Location _____

Account Number _____

Contact Person _____

Documentation Location _____

Notes _____

_____

Type _____

Location _____

Account Number _____

Contact Person _____

Documentation Location _____

Notes _____

_____

Investments: Stocks, Mutual Funds, and Other

Type

Location

Account Number

Contact Person

Documentation Location

Notes

Type

Location

Account Number

Contact Person

Documentation Location

Notes

Type

Location

Account Number

Contact Person

Documentation Location

Notes

Assets Overview

Investments: Stocks, Mutual Funds, and Other

Type

Location

Account Number

Contact Person

Documentation Location

Notes

Type

Location

Account Number

Contact Person

Documentation Location

Notes

Type

Location

Account Number

Contact Person

Documentation Location

Notes

Insurance Benefits

Policy Type

Location

Account Number

Contact Person

Documentation Location

Notes

Policy Type

Location

Account Number

Contact Person

Documentation Location

Notes

Policy Type

Location

Account Number

Contact Person

Documentation Location

Notes

Insurance Benefits

Policy Type

Location

Account Number

Contact Person

Documentation Location

Notes

Policy Type

Location

Account Number

Contact Person

Documentation Location

Notes

Policy Type

Location

Account Number

Contact Person

Documentation Location

Notes

Assets Overview

Employer Benefits #1

Name

Account Number

Contact Person

Documentation Location

Notes

Employer Benefits #2

Name

Account Number

Contact Person

Documentation Location

Notes

Employer Benefits #3

Name

Account Number

Contact Person

Documentation Location

Notes

Retirement Benefits

Name ....

Account Number ....

Contact Person ....

Documentation Location ....

Notes ....

....

Retirement Benefits #2

Name ....

Account Number ....

Contact Person ....

Documentation Location ....

Notes ....

....

Social Security

Name ....

Account Number ....

Contact Person ....

Documentation Location ....

Notes ....

....

Assets Overview

Other: *Veteran's Benefits, Etc.*

Name _____

Account Number _____

Contact Person _____

Documentation Location _____

Notes _____

_____

Other

Name _____

Account Number _____

Contact Person _____

Documentation Location _____

Notes _____

_____

Other

Name _____

Account Number _____

Contact Person _____

Documentation Location _____

Notes _____

_____

Other - Money Owed to Me

Name

Account Number

Contact Person

Documentation Location

Notes

Name

Account Number

Contact Person

Documentation Location

Notes

Name

Account Number

Contact Person

Documentation Location

Notes

Assets Overview

Personal Items, Jewelry, and Heirlooms

Item

Location

Notes

Item

Location

Notes

Item

Location

Notes

Item

Location

Notes

45

Personal Items, Jewelry, and Heirlooms

Item

Location

Notes

Item

Location

Notes

Item

Location

Notes

Item

Location

Notes

Personal Items, Jewelry, and Heirlooms

Item

Location

Notes

Item

Location

Notes

Item

Location

Notes

Item

Location

Notes

Personal Items, Jewelry, and Heirlooms

Item

Location

Notes

Item

Location

Notes

Item

Location

Notes

Item

Location

Notes

Personal Items, Jewelry, and Heirlooms

Item

Location

Notes

Item

Location

Notes

Item

Location

Notes

Item

Location

Notes

Personal Items, Jewelry, and Heirlooms

Item

Location

Notes

Item

Location

Notes

Item

Location

Notes

Item

Location

Notes

Storage: Company Name

Address

Key Location or Combination Number

Storage: Company Name

Address

Key Location or Combination Number

Notes and Instructions

Business Information

Business Details

Business Name _____

BusinesType _____

Address _____

_____

Landlord Name _____

Contact Information _____

Lease Documentation Location _____

Partner / Co-Owner Name _____

Contact Information _____

Partner / Co-Owner Name _____

Contact Information _____

Partner / Co-Owner Name _____

Contact Information _____

Partner / Co-Owner Name _____

Contact Information _____

Keys Location _____

Notes _____

_____

Associates, Employees, and Contractors

Name

Contact Information

Name

Contact Information

Name

Contact Information

Name

Contact Information

Name

Contact Information

Name

Contact Information

Name

Contact Information

Name

Contact Information

Notes

Business Information

Name

Contact Information

Name

Contact Information

Name

Contact Information

Name

Contact Information

Name

Contact Information

Name

Contact Information

Name

Contact Information

Name

Contact Information

Name

Contact Information

Notes

Business Information

Bank Name

Address

Contact Information

Business Bank Account Number

Business Bank Account Number

Credit Card Number

Username / PIN

Credit Card Number

Username / PIN

Documentation Location

Notes

Bank Name

Address

Contact Information

Business Bank Account Number

Business Bank Account Number

Credit Card Number

Username / PIN

Credit Card Number

Username / PIN

Documentation Location

Notes

Accountant Name

Contact Information

Lawyer

Contact Information

Insurance Agency / Agent

Contact Information

Notes on Income, Royalties, Key Accounts Etc.

Business Website Name

Hosting Provider

Username and Password

Website Developer Name

Contact Information

Documentation Location

Online Income Stream #1

Online Income Stream #2

Partner / Co-Owner Name

Contact Information

Partner / Co-Owner Name

Contact Information

Partner / Co-Owner Name

Contact Information

Business Email Address Name

Username and Password

Business Email Address Name

Username and Password

Business Email Address Name

Username and Password

Notes

Online Business Information

Notes: *Instructions for Domain Name Renewal, Hosting, Expenses, Etc.*

Notes: *Instructions for Domain Name Renewal, Monthly Hosting and Expenses, Etc.*

Social Media

Name

Username and Password

Name

Username and Password

Name

Username and Password

Name

Username and Password

Name

Username and Password

Name

Username and Password

Name

Username and Password

Name

Username and Password

Name

Username and Password

Name

Username and Password

Online Business Information

Accounts

Name

Username and Password

Name

Username and Password

Name

Username and Password

Name

Username and Password

Name

Username and Password

Name

Username and Password

Name

Username and Password

Name

Username and Password

Name

Username and Password

Name

Username and Password

Online Business Information

Accounts

Name

Username and Password

Name

Username and Password

Name

Username and Password

Name

Username and Password

Name

Username and Password

Name

Username and Password

Name

Username and Password

Name

Username and Password

Name

Username and Password

Name

Username and Password

Money I Owe to Others

Person / Company Name _____

Contact Information _____

Documentation Location _____

Notes _____

_____

Person / Company Name _____

Contact Information _____

Documentation Location _____

Notes _____

_____

Person / Company Name _____

Contact Information _____

Documentation Location _____

Notes _____

_____

Person / Company Name _____

Contact Information _____

Documentation Location _____

Notes _____

_____

Additional Details _____

_____

Instructions

Banking Information

Bank Name

Account Type and Number

Account Type and Number

Bank Online Web Address

Username and Password

Debit Card Number

Credit Card Number

CV and Password

Online Username and Password

Rewards

Notes

Bank Name

Account Type and Number

Account Type and Number

Bank Online Web Address

Username and Password

Debit Card Number

Credit Card Number

CV and Password

Online Username and Password

Rewards

Notes

Banking Information

Account Type and Number ....

Account Type and Number ....

Bank Online Web Address ....

Username and Password ....

Debit Card Number ....

Credit Card Number ....

CV and Password ....

Online Username and Password ....

Rewards ....

Notes ....

Safe Deposit Box

Bank Location ....

Box Number ....

Key Location ....

Contents ....

....

....

Safe Deposit Box

Bank Location ....

Box Number ....

Key Location ....

Contents ....

....

....

Banking Information

Other Cards: *Credit, Line of Credit, Department Stores, Etc.*

Name

Account Number

Online Website

Username and Password

Name

Account Number

Online Website

Username and Password

Name

Account Number

Online Website

Username and Password

Name

Account Number

Online Website

Username and Password

Name

Account Number

Online Website

Username and Password

Notes

Banking Information

Other Cards: *Credit, Line of Credit, Department Stores, Etc.*

Name

Account Number

Online Website

Username and Password

Name

Account Number

Online Website

Username and Password

Name

Account Number

Online Website

Username and Password

Name

Account Number

Online Website

Username and Password

Name

Account Number

Online Website

Username and Password

Notes

Banking Information

Other Cards: *Credit, Line of Credit, Department Stores, Etc.*

Name

Account Number

Online Website

Username and Password

Name

Account Number

Online Website

Username and Password

Name

Account Number

Online Website

Username and Password

Name

Account Number

Online Website

Username and Password

Name

Account Number

Online Website

Username and Password

Notes

Banking Information

Mortgage, Line of Credit, Loans

Mortgage Details

Bank / Lender

Contact Information

Account Number

Documentation Location

Mortgage Details

Bank / Lender

Contact Information

Account Number

Documentation Location

Second Mortgage Details

Bank / Lender

Contact Information

Account Number

Documentation Location

Bank / Lender

Contact Information

Account Number

Documentation Location

Notes

Banking Information

Line of Credit

Bank / Lender

Contact Information

Account Number

Documentation Location

Line of Credit

Bank / Lender

Contact Information

Account Number

Documentation Location

Other

Lender

Contact Information

Account Number

Documentation Location

Other

Lender

Contact Information

Account Number

Documentation Location

Notes

Banking Information

Loans: *Cars, Student Loan, Etc.*

Bank / Lender

Contact Information

Account Number

Documentation Location

Bank / Lender

Contact Information

Account Number

Documentation Location

Bank / Lender

Contact Information

Account Number

Documentation Location

Bank / Lender

Contact Information

Account Number

Documentation Location

Bank / Lender

Contact Information

Account Number

Documentation Location

Notes

Important Documents Location

Will Location

_____

_____

Notes _____

Health Care Power of Attorney Documentation Location

_____

_____

Notes _____

Passport Location

_____

_____

Notes _____

Birth Certificate Location

_____

_____

Notes _____

Social Security Number Location

Notes

Drivers Licence Location

Notes

Marriage Certificate

Notes

Tax Documents Location

Notes

Divorce Papers Location

Notes

Life Insurance Location

Notes

Health Insurance Location - Medical

Notes

Health Insurance Location – Dental

Notes

Health Insurance Location - Vision

Notes

Health Insurance Location – Funeral / Other

Notes

Vehicle Insurance Location

Notes

Vehicle Insurance Location #2

Notes

Vehicle Insurance Location #3

Notes

Home Owner Insurance Location

Notes

Rental Home Insurance Location

Notes

Children's Insurance Location

Notes

Additional Family / Dependents Insurance Location

Notes

Pet Insurance Location

Notes

Pet Insurance

Notes

Storage Insurance

Notes

Other

_____

Notes _____

Other

_____

Notes _____

Other

_____

Notes _____

Other

_____

Notes _____

Other

_____

Notes _____

Insurance Information

Health Insurance

Company Name

Agents Name

Contact Information

HSA (Health Savings Account) Information

Health Insurance - Dental

Company Name

Agents Name

Contact Information

Health Insurance – Vision

Company Name

Agents Name

Contact Information

Health Insurance – Medical / Other

Company Name

Agents Name

Contact Information

Life Insurance

Company Name _____

Agents Name _____

Contact Information _____

Funeral Insurance

Company Name _____

Agents Name _____

Contact Information _____

Vehicle Insurance

Company Name _____

Agents Name _____

Contact Information _____

Vehicle Insurance

Company Name _____

Agents Name _____

Contact Information _____

Vehicle Insurance

Company Name _____

Agents Name _____

Contact Information _____

Insurance Information

Home Owners Insurance

Company Name

Agents Name

Contact Information

Rental Home Insurance

Company Name

Agents Name

Contact Information

Children's Insurance

Company Name

Agents Name

Contact Information

Children's Insurance

Company Name

Agents Name

Contact Information

Children's Insurance

Company Name

Agents Name

Contact Information

Other Dependents Insurance

Company Name

Agents Name

Contact Information

Other Dependents Insurance

Company Name

Agents Name

Contact Information

Pet Insurance

Company Name

Agents Name

Contact Information

Pet Insurance

Company Name

Agents Name

Contact Information

Storage Insurance

Company Name

Agents Name

Contact Information

Other Insurance

Company Name ....

Agents Name ....

Contact Information ....

Other Insurance

Company Name ....

Agents Name ....

Contact Information ....

Other Insurance

Company Name ....

Agents Name ....

Contact Information ....

Other Insurance

Company Name ....

Agents Name ....

Contact Information ....

Other Insurance

Company Name ....

Agents Name ....

Contact Information ....

Insurance Information - Notes

Medical Information

Health Care Power of Attorney

Name

Contact Information

Do Not Resuscitate Instructions Document Location

Organ Donor Instructions Document Location

Blood Type

Primary Care Physician

Name

Contact Information

Address

Medical Conditions

_____

_____

_____

_____

_____

_____

_____

_____

Medications

_____

_____

_____

_____

_____

_____

_____

_____

Medical Information

Allergies, Food Sensitivity, and Reactions

If Incapacitated Please Follow Below Requests (Further Details in DNR Document)

Medical Information

Preferred Hospital

Name _____

Contact Information _____

Address _____

_____

Pharmacy

Name _____

Contact Information _____

Address _____

_____

Caregiver Company / Person

Name _____

Contact Information _____

Address _____

_____

Caregiver Company / Person

Name _____

Contact Information _____

Address _____

_____

Dependents Instructions for Care

My Dependents

Name

Relationship

Contact Information

Personal Documentation Location

Health Conditions Documentation Location

Guardianship Instructions Documentation Location

Guardian Name

Contact Information

Primary Care Physician

Contact Information

Notes

My Dependents

Name

Relationship

Contact Information

Personal Documentation Location

Health Conditions Documentation Location

Guardianship Instructions Documentation Location

Guardian Name

Contact Information

Primary Care Physician

Contact Information

Notes

My Dependents

Name

Relationship

Contact Information

Personal Documentation Location

Health Conditions Documentation Location

Guardianship Instructions Documentation Location

Guardian Name

Contact Information

Primary Care Physician

Contact Information

Notes

My Dependents

Name

Relationship

Contact Information

Personal Documentation Location

Health Conditions Documentation Location

Guardianship Instructions Documentation Location

Guardian Name

Contact Information

Primary Care Physician

Contact Information

Notes

My Dependents

Name _____

Relationship _____

Contact Information _____

Personal Documentation Location _____

_____

Health Conditions Documentation Location_ _____

_____

_____

Guardianship Instructions Documentation Location _____

_____

Guardian Name _____

Contact Information _____

_____

_____

Primary Care Physician _____

Contact Information _____

Notes _____

_____

_____

My Dependents

Name

Relationship

Contact Information

Personal Documentation Location

Health Conditions Documentation Location

Guardianship Instructions Documentation Location

Guardian Name

Contact Information

Primary Care Physician

Contact Information

Notes

My Dependents – Pets

Name / Type of Pet

Name of Veterinarian

Contact Information

Address

License, Insurance, and Documentation Location

Health Conditions

Medications

Guardianship Instructions Documentation Location

Guardian Name

Contact Information

General Instructions of Care – Food, Habits, Exercise, Sleep, and Other Needs

My Dependents – Pets

Name / Type of Pet _____

Name of Veterinarian _____

Contact Information _____

Address _____

_____

License, Insurance, and Documentation Location _____

_____

Health Conditions _____

_____

_____

Medications _____

_____

_____

Guardianship Instructions Documentation Location _____

_____

Guardian Name _____

Contact Information _____

General Instructions of Care – Food, Habits, Exercise, Sleep, and Other Needs

_____

_____

_____

_____

_____

_____

My Dependents – Pets

Name / Type of Pet _____

Name of Veterinarian _____

Contact Information _____

Address _____

_____

License, Insurance, and Documentation Location _____

_____

Health Conditions _____

_____

_____

Medications _____

_____

_____

Guardianship Instructions Documentation Location _____

_____

Guardian Name _____

Contact Information _____

General Instructions of Care – Food, Habits, Exercise, Sleep, and Other Needs

_____

_____

_____

_____

_____

_____

My Dependents – Notes

My Dependents – Notes

Loose Ends to Tie Up

Follow Up: Cancel, Close, Pay, Change of Name, Etc.

Example: Hydro, Electric, Phone, Cable, Internet, Storage, Credit Cards, Autopay, Banking...

Company / Contact Information

Account Number

Username and Password

Notes

Company / Contact Information

Account Number

Username and Password

Notes

Company / Contact Information

Account Number

Username and Password

Notes

Company / Contact Information

Account Number

Username and Password

Notes

Loose Ends to Tie Up

Company / Contact Information

Account Number

Username and Password

Notes

Company / Contact Information

Account Number

Username and Password

Notes

Company / Contact Information

Account Number

Username and Password

Notes

Company / Contact Information

Account Number

Username and Password

Notes

Company / Contact Information

Account Number

Username and Password

Notes

Loose Ends to Tie Up

Company / Contact Information ....

Account Number ....

Username and Password ....

Notes ....

Company / Contact Information ....

Account Number ....

Username and Password ....

Notes ....

Company / Contact Information ....

Account Number ....

Username and Password ....

Notes ....

Company / Contact Information ....

Account Number ....

Username and Password ....

Notes ....

Company / Contact Information ....

Account Number ....

Username and Password ....

Notes ....

Loose Ends to Tie Up

Company / Contact Information

Account Number

Username and Password

Notes

Company / Contact Information

Account Number

Username and Password

Notes

Company / Contact Information

Account Number

Username and Password

Notes

Company / Contact Information

Account Number

Username and Password

Notes

Company / Contact Information

Account Number

Username and Password

Notes

Loose Ends to Tie Up

Company / Contact Information

Account Number

Username and Password

Notes

Company / Contact Information

Account Number

Username and Password

Notes

Company / Contact Information

Account Number

Username and Password

Notes

Company / Contact Information

Account Number

Username and Password

Notes

Company / Contact Information

Account Number

Username and Password

Notes

Loose Ends to Tie Up – Online

Example: Email, Website, Hosting, Social Media, Banking, Amazon and eBay Memberships

Company / Website

Account Number

Username and Password

Notes

Company / Website

Account Number

Username and Password

Notes

Company / Website

Account Number

Username and Password

Notes

Company / Website

Account Number

Username and Password

Notes

Loose Ends to Tie Up – Online

Company / Website

Account Number

Username and Password

Notes

Company / Website

Account Number

Username and Password

Notes

Company / Website

Account Number

Username and Password

Notes

Company / Website

Account Number

Username and Password

Notes

Company / Website

Account Number

Username and Password

Notes

Company / Website

Account Number

Username and Password

Notes

Company / Website

Account Number

Username and Password

Notes

Company / Website

Account Number

Username and Password

Notes

Company / Website

Account Number

Username and Password

Notes

Company / Website

Account Number

Username and Password

Notes

Company / Website

Account Number

Username and Password

Notes

Company / Website

Account Number

Username and Password

Notes

Loose Ends to Tie Up — Online

Company / Website

Account Number

Username and Password

Notes

Company / Website

Account Number

Username and Password

Notes

Company / Website

Account Number

Username and Password

Notes

Company / Website

Account Number

Username and Password

Notes

Final Wishes and Instructions

Final Wishes and Instructions

Final Wishes and Instructions

Final Wishes and Instructions

A Personal Message for My Loved Ones

A Personal Message for:

A Personal Message for:

A Personal Message for:

A Personal Message for:

A Personal Message for:

A Personal Message for:

A Personal Message for:

A Personal Message for:

A Personal Message for:

Notes

Notes

Notes

Notes

My Final Farewell

_____

_____

_____

_____

_____

_____

_____

_____

Signature

_____

Name and Date

_____